GARDEN PLAN

BARRINGTON·COVRT
·SOMERSET·

·FOR·LIEVT·COL· A·ARTHVR·LYLE·

JAN 1917

The National Trust

## The Glory of Somerset

Barrington Court today is an intimate family garden, inspired by one of the greatest British garden designers, Gertrude Jekyll. Her love of graduated colour effects, of enclosed 'outdoor rooms' and open vistas, of hard features and soft planting – all can be found here. They also provide the perfect setting for the old manor house, which was built in the 1550s from golden Ham Hill stone. Next to it stands the contrasting red-brick Strode House, which was put up a hundred years later as grand stables. It all seems to tell a story of continuity and contentment over four centuries.

But in 1907, when the National Trust acquired Barrington Court as its first country house, the scene was rather different. The windows of the Great Hall were bricked up and chickens were roosting inside. The old gardens had disappeared, and the house was surrounded by a sad jumble of dilapidated farm buildings.

Thanks to a generous benefactor, to three generations of the Lyle family (tenants from 1920 to 1991), their architect, J.E. Forbes, and a devoted garden staff, the house was saved, and the magnificent Jekyll garden was created as the focus of a model estate.

More is being done all the time to fulfil the ambitious plans of the Lyle family and Gertrude Jekyll for the garden and to ensure the long-term financial security of the whole estate. But Barrington can justly reclaim its old title: 'The Glory of Somerset'.

(*Above*) The south front of Barrington Court, which was built in the mid-16th century

*Clematis montana* 'Rubens' smothers the entrance to the Lily Garden, while the beds below are filled with red and yellow wall-flowers, yellow alyssum and purple pansies

'Iceberg' roses grow up the walls of the White Garden

# The History of Barrington Court

*Henry Daubeney*

There has been a house on this site since Domesday. In 1514 the estate was inherited by Henry Daubeney, who followed his father into royal service. Determined to make his mark, he paraded his servants and 80 horses in full livery through the streets of London. He finally achieved his life's ambition in 1538, when he was created Earl of Bridgwater, and he may have begun building the present house as a grand country seat befitting his new status. However, he was soon bankrupted by his ambitions and fell from power with the disgrace of Catherine Howard in 1541. According to a contemporary, at his death in 1548 there was 'no means to buy fire or candles or to bury him but what was done in charity by his sister'.

*The Cliftons and the Strodes*

William Clifton, a wealthy London merchant, bought the estate in 1552 and completed the house by 1559. Three generations of Cliftons lived at Barrington until 1605, when it was sold to Sir Thomas Phelips, a member of the family that had built nearby Montacute in the previous decade. It was sold again in 1625 to William Strode, a clothier from Shepton Mallet who had made his fortune from trade and a judicious marriage to a local heiress, Joan Barnard of Downside; their coats of arms appear in the overmantel of an upstairs bedroom. He is said to have 'bestowed money and labour to restore [the house] to its pristine beauty'.

His son, William Strode II, went a step further, building the massive stable block which bears his initials in 1674. A fervent Presbyterian and MP for Ilchester in 1679, he entertained his supporters 'with his great treats in the town and large invitations of his party to his house in Barrington'. The following year he welcomed a far more dangerous guest, the Duke of Monmouth, whose attempt to overthrow James II in 1685 ended in bloody defeat at the Battle of Sedgemoor seven miles north of Barrington.

*Decline*

The estate passed out of the Strode family in 1745 and through many different hands over the next 100 years. By the mid-19th century it had declined to the status of a tenanted farmhouse, and only the west wing was inhabited. Things went from bad to worse with the agricultural depression of the 1870s: more and more of the decorative fittings were torn out and sold, the windows were boarded over, and the surviving shell became little better than a cattle barn.

By the 1890s the plight of ancient manor houses like Barrington was provoking increasing concern. As Frank Webb, a nephew of the tenant, remembered: 'People came many miles to view the old place with its ample corridors, dark cells, oaken wainscotting, numerous attics ..., its quaint staircases and its pleasant surroundings.' Among these visitors was Canon Hardwicke Rawnsley, one of the founders of the National Trust. After a large jug of the local cider, he was taken round, finding the attics full of owls, which 'make a noise at night as if people were shuffling about and dragging weights over the rough boarding'. Despite the building's pitiful state, he was won over by the sense of light and grace, and recommended that the Trust acquire it.

The red-brick Strode House was built by William Strode II in 1674 as stables and now forms a stunning backdrop to the garden

The multi-faceted heraldic sundial on the South Lawn

The south front in 1904, when the windows of the Great Hall had been bricked up and the house was in a semi-derelict state

The Court being repaired in the early 1920s

'Mr Cube' was invented in the 1940s by Tate & Lyle as part of a successful campaign to stop the government nationalising the sugar industry

Gertrude Jekyll; painted by William Nicholson in 1920, around the time she was consulted by the Lyles (National Portrait Gallery)

## The National Trust

When the Trust took on Barrington Court, it was only twelve years old and still a tiny organisation. The bill for purchase and initial repairs came to £11,500, most of which was met by Miss J.L. Woodward; the rest was raised fairly quickly by a public appeal. Paying for Barrington's upkeep was to prove a much bigger headache. Indeed, for the next 30 years, whenever the Trust contemplated acquiring another big house, the cry went up: 'Remember Barrington!'

## The Lyle Family: Creating a Model Estate

So the Trust was delighted when Colonel Arthur Lyle, a director of the famous sugar-refining company Tate & Lyle, agreed to take a 99-year lease on the house in 1920. He had been badly wounded at the Battle of the Somme in 1916 and was keen to move to the West Country from his home in Buckinghamshire. He was also looking for somewhere to install the collection of historic woodwork he had salvaged from houses like Barrington. Barrington was recommended to Colonel Lyle by an architect friend, J.E. Forbes, who prepared a detailed master plan for remodelling the Court, the Strode House and the surrounding landscape. Derelict farm buildings were cleared away from the north side of the house to create a spacious forecourt and approach avenue, leading to a row of cottages built by Forbes from local stone in a mellow Arts and Crafts style. Barrington became the centre of a model estate with new farm buildings, a house for the agent (Captain Beacham, a fearsome ex-Coldstream Guards officer), a racquets court and kennels (now the visitor reception area).

Around the house Forbes conceived a complex scheme of walled gardens, of a kind that might have surrounded it in Elizabethan times. He also asked the famous garden designer Gertrude Jekyll for her advice on planting. Biscuit tins of the limy soil were sent to her, and although she was in her late seventies and almost blind, just by crumbling the earth between her fingers she was able to tell what would grow best. Colonel Lyle's wife, Elsie, who was a keen plantswoman, also visited Miss Jekyll at Munstead to discuss the plans. In the event, only Forbes and Jekyll's scheme for the area to the west of the Strode House was carried out in full, but the Lily and Rose and Iris Gardens still give a very vivid picture of what they had in mind.

Col Lyle was succeeded in 1931 by his son Ian, who became Chairman of Tate & Lyle and was knighted in 1959. During the Second World War the Court was occupied

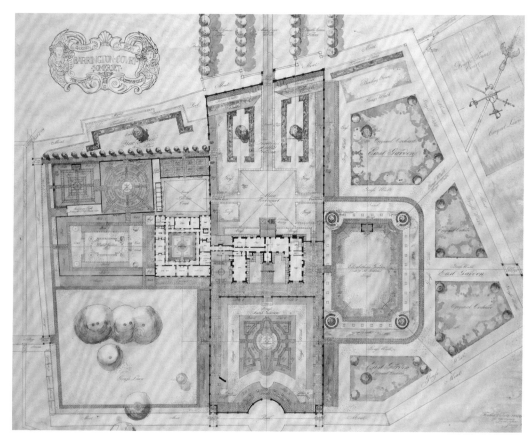

(*Above*) The Strode House under repair in the early 1920s

Forbes's 1917 master plan for Barrington Court. Only the proposals for the gardens to the west (left) of the Strode House were carried out

by a boys' prep school, the family retreated to the Strode House, and the Home Guard drilled in the squash court, but the garden came through more or less intact. In the post-war years Sir Ian and his head gardener Harry Burton created an arboretum from the old cider orchard to the east of the house. On Sir Ian's death in 1978 much of the family furniture left the house, and so in 1986 his son Andrew invited Stuart Interiors Ltd to furnish the empty rooms in the Court with reproduction pieces. With his head gardener Christine Brain he continued to develop the garden with new planting schemes inspired by Forbes and Jekyll's ideas. However, by 1991 the cost of maintaining the house and garden had become so high that he decided to give up the lease to the National Trust, which now manages the estate.

# Tour of the House and Garden

## Barrington Court (1)

Barrington adopted the typical 'E' plan of early Elizabethan country houses. Outside, symmetry reigns, but oddly positioned windows hint at the unsymmetrical medieval arrangement within: a Great Hall on the east side separated by a screens passage from smaller service rooms on the west. Masons' marks found on much of the beautiful Ham Hill stonework suggest that the building was largely constructed in the 1550s by William Clifton. Like the contemporary Parnham Hall in Dorset, it is embellished with buttresses at the corners of the wings and a forest of twisted finials on the roof (restored in 1968, thanks to the generosity of Sir Ian Lyle). The projecting wings, porch, staircase towers and roof gables give a subtle rhythm to the south front. The north front, which Forbes turned into the entrance, is altogether plainer and less fun.

Of the original interior almost nothing remains: not a door, not even the staircase, was spared. The Lyles revealed the mid-16th-century minstrels' gallery and linenfold panelling in the Great Hall, and put in a sprung floor for dancing. They employed Scottish craftsmen to build a new staircase, which includes some early 17th-century banisters and the bottom newel post, but it is mostly modern oak sandblasted to look old. They also installed a genuine Tudor ceiling above it.

## The Strode House (2)

This was built in contrasting red brick by William Strode in 1674 to provide stabling for twelve horses and shelter for two coaches. It was open on the north side until 1920, when Forbes converted it into a family home for the Lyles, adding the chimneystacks and a kitchen in the new north range. It now houses the National Trust restaurant and shop on the ground floor, and four apartments on the first floor.

## The Chestnut Avenues (3)

The avenues of chestnuts which meet in front of the house were the first part of the park to be planted by the Lyles. Over the last 70 years they have gradually been thinned so that the magnificent mature trees now stand about eighteen metres apart.

## The Lime Walk (4), East Orchard (5) and South Lawn (6)

Forbes and Jekyll planned a formal 'Elizabethan Garden' to the east of the Court, with parterres picked out in grey-, purple- and white-flowered plants. The Lyles, however, decided to leave this as a traditional Somerset cider orchard until 1951, when Sir Ian laid out the Lime Walk as a vista aligned with the east front and flanked by an arboretum containing fine specimen maples, beeches, cypresses and junipers. Forbes and Jekyll had equally ambitious ideas for the south side of the house, but again the Lyles were concerned that they might detract from the splendour of the house, and so left this as an expanse of grass.

The result is an attractive contrast between open simplicity to the east of the Court and enclosed complexity to the west, very much the hallmark of Arts and Crafts thinking.

The Strode House from the Lily Garden

Cider apples in the East Orchard

An aerial view from the north in the 1970s, showing the chestnut avenues which link the Court with the thatched cottages on the estate

Red-hot pokers (*Kniphofia*) in the Lily Garden. The planting here is predominantly red and orange

*Helenium* in the Lily Garden

### The South Border (7)

The rich, L-shaped border which runs along the south wall of the Lily Garden overlooking the South Lawn is filled with shrubs and hardy perennials in soft shades of purple and pink, such as the Smoke Bush (*Cotinus coggygria*), *Daphne* x *burkwoodii* and wisteria. The brick path provides a visual link with the Strode House and is a source of interest in its own right, having been laid in an imaginative range of different patterns.

### The Lily Garden (8)

This is the largest of the enclosed flower gardens and the first to be created following Gertrude Jekyll's plans. She got the idea of placing a lily pond in the centre of a formal garden from Italy. In *Wall and Water Gardens* (1901) she explained how the beautifully coloured forms of the new water lily varieties 'would exactly accord with masonry of the highest refinement, and with the feeling of repose that is suggested by a surface of still water'. Forbes and Jekyll had envisaged a sunken lawn around the pool, but this would have involved expensive excavation. A similar effect was created more simply by raising the terrace and the beds instead.

Gertrude Jekyll is best known today for her love of pale shades, but she also used strong colours: the key was to get the relationship between the individual blooms right. The palette starts with fiery orange, scarlet and crimson near the red-brick walls of the Strode House, fading away to pale pink, yellow and white at the opposite end of the garden, and rising back again to orange as the border returns towards the house. This almost symphonic effect is achieved with azaleas, yuccas, day lilies, heliotropes and *Crinum* x *powellii* (the last the only survival of the original planting). The outer borders are planted at the back with warm-coloured dahlias, *Canna* 'Roi Humbert', red-hot pokers and *Helenium*, while dark foliage shrubs and climbers scramble up the surrounding walls.

### The White Garden (9)

Within the old farmyard walls Forbes and Jekyll devised a rose and peony garden. In the centre is a statue of a dancing faun which the Lyles had brought from their garden at Beel House in Buckinghamshire. By 1986, the roses had grown tired, and it was decided to create a completely new garden, using the original wheel-shaped arrangement of beds. In her influential book *Colour in the Flower Garden* (1908), Miss Jekyll had advocated the idea of an all-white garden, which was to be made famous by Vita Sackville-West at Sissinghurst in the 1950s.

The white-, cream- and silver-flowering plants – annuals in the central beds and the herbaceous perennials in the outer borders – have been carefully chosen for the amount of sun and shade they receive. In the sunnier, south-facing positions are *Lychnis coronaria* 'Alba' and *Lysimachia clethroïdes*, while the more shaded beds facing north are filled with *Polygonum biflorum*. Contrasts of scale and texture are also important, with *Stachys* and *Viola septentrionalis* at the front, and *Crambe cordifolia* and *Campanula lactiflora alba* providing height at the back of the outside borders.

In mid-summer, when the White Garden is at its best, the overall effect is splendidly blowsy and Edwardian.

The White Garden in mid-summer

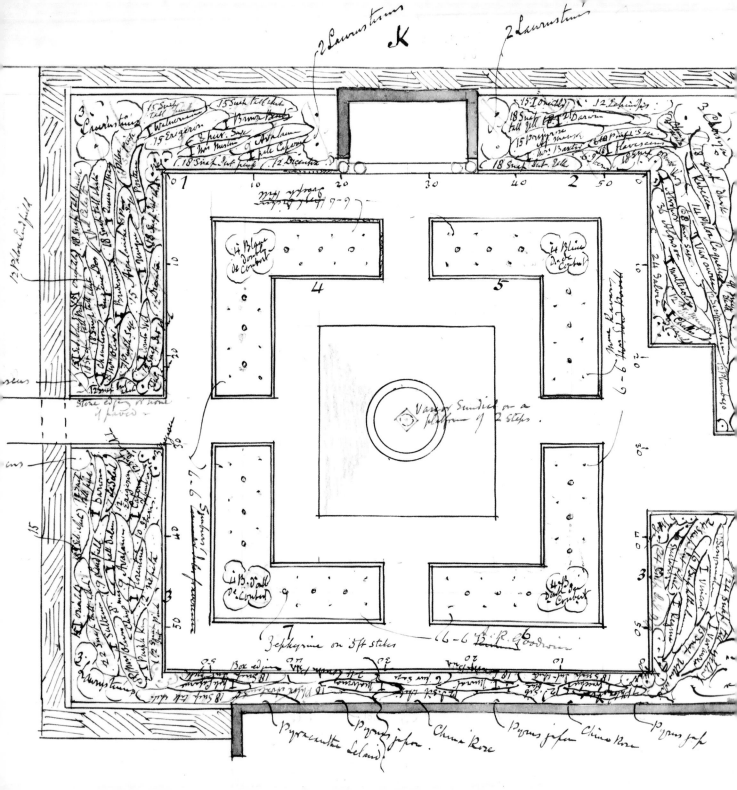

## Bustalls (10)

The name comes from the pens which were built in the early 19th century for rearing veal calves. Forbes's plan envisaged moving them, but they were retained to form an unusual backdrop for a long border stretching from the west moat to the entrance drive from the Strode House. Here Elsie Lyle grew sweet peas and other cut flowers for the house. The rectangular beds beyond to the west are given over to mixed planting, including the rose 'Roseraie de l'Haÿ'.

## The Rose and Iris Garden (11)

Miss Jekyll planned to fill the outer borders with bearded irises in a wide range of colours, punctuated with phlox and French and African marigolds, with her favourite *Saxifraga umbrosa* and *Bergenia cordifolia* providing a frame of darker evergreen at the front. She suggested the roses 'Zéphirine Drouhin' and 'Blanche Double de Coubert'

for the inner L-shaped beds, which have been replanted recently using equivalent modern varieties.

Old varieties of bearded iris are interspersed with herbaceous plants, purple sage and bold plantings of antirrhinums to give a vivid colour scheme through the summer months.

## The Pergola Walk (12)

Brick and wood pergolas were a favourite Jekyll feature. This one was designed in her style by Andrew Lyle and Christine Brain in 1981 to cover the path from the Bustalls to the White Garden. The climbers include honeysuckle, wisteria, jasmine, hop and clematises such as 'Perle d'Azur' and 'Nelly Moser', while the flanking borders are filled with hellebores, spurge and geranium, which bring a splash of colour to the garden in the quiet period between the daffodils and the first of the summer borders.

The Pergola Walk, which is hung with wisteria blossom in early summer

(*Far left*) The 19th-century cattle pens, or bustalls, provide an unusual support for *Clematis macropetala* 'Markham's Pink'

(*Left*) Bearded irises in the Rose and Iris Garden

(*Opposite*) Gertrude Jekyll's planting plan for the Rose and Iris Garden, which has been used as the basis for the recent replanting

## The Moat (13)

The doorway at the end of the Pergola Walk leads through the outer garden wall and on to a wooden bridge spanning the moat. Forbes dug out a humble drainage ditch to form the moat, which runs around two sides of the walled gardens and was intended to evoke the Elizabethan origins of Barrington Court.

## The Kitchen Garden (14)

Traditionally, every country house estate had a kitchen garden which made it almost self-sufficient in fruit and vegetables. Sadly, many have disappeared under grass in the 20th century. At Barrington, however, the superb 1920s scheme remains defiantly in cultivation, supplying food for the restaurant, plants for sale, and an occasional opportunity for visitors to 'pick their own' in season.

The carved stone fruit and vegetables over the entrance doorways announce what lies within. The main area is divided into four beds by broad paths which meet at a statue of a boy with a swan. A wide range of soft fruit and vegetables is grown within the mellow Barrington stone walls built by Forbes and now covered with espalier-, fan- and cordon-trained fruit trees. The huge clay pots are used for forcing rhubarb and sea-kale. The southern section of the garden is given over to glasshouses and a plant sales area (15).

## The Herbaceous Border (16)

Beyond the moat is a stone building with a picturesque hipped roof and dormer windows which looks old and rustic, but in fact was built in 1920 to house the Lyles' racquets court. It now provides a focal point for the deep border which stretches away along the outer wall of the Kitchen Garden. This was the brainchild of Elsie Lyle, the gardening expert of the family. Her roses have now mainly been replaced by herbaceous plants: *Bergenia cordifolia, Iberis sempervirens and Helianthemum* at the front, *Eryngium, Veronica* and *Erigeron* in the middle, and *Alcea rosea, Solidago, Helenium* and asters at the back.

Michaelmas daisies in the Herbaceous Border

Marjoram, Welsh onions and lovage in the Kitchen Garden

Cabbages in the Kitchen Garden

The Herbaceous Border